More
48-Hour Afghans

by Jean Leinhauser and Rita Weiss

Leisure Arts, Inc.,
Maumelle, Arkansas

PRODUCED BY

PRODUCTION TEAM

Creative Directors: Jean Leinhauser
and Rita Weiss

Senior Technical Editor: Ellen W. Liberles

Photographer: Carol Wilson Mansfield

Pattern Testers: Kimberly Britt, Ann Chubb,
Tammy Hebert, Patricia Honaker, and
Tracy Pokrzywa

Book Design: Linda Causee

PUBLISHED BY LEISURE ARTS

© 2011 by Leisure Arts, Inc.,
104 Champs Blvd., Ste. 100,
Little Rock, AR 72113

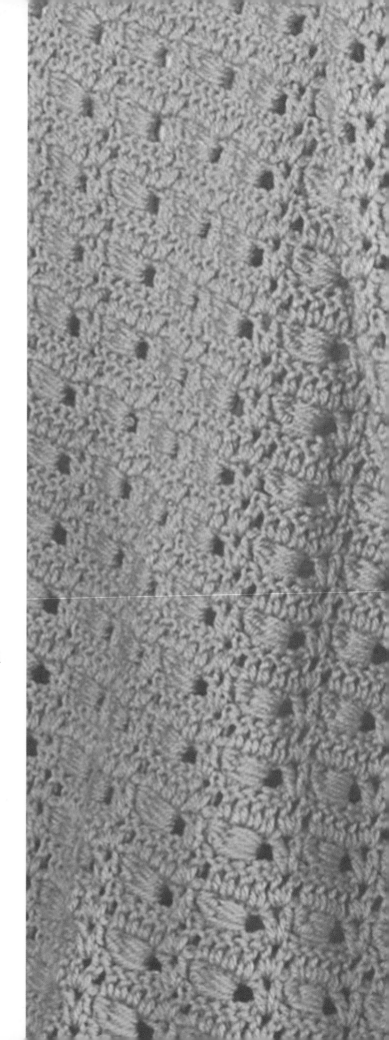

INTRODUCTION

Several years ago we produced a collection of 48-hour crocheted afghans. We were amazed and delighted with the response. The concept of making an afghan in 48 hours appealed to so many crocheters, and your emails and letters encouraged us to give you more. So here is a brand new collection of some of our favorite 48-hour afghans.

We know that crocheters are passionate about their hooks, about the yarns they choose, about the patterns they prefer and what they enjoy making. And that favorite project is – afghans! Perhaps it is the endless variety of designs and colors that afghans can display, and certainly it is also because crocheters are givers.

Most crocheters are generous, giving away most of what they make. Somebody getting married, having a baby, going off to college, going through a hard time? Time to make an afghan! We know that crocheters readily create and send their beautiful afghans all over the world where warmth and comfort are needed. Wherever there is an earthquake, a flood or other disaster, crocheters get their hooks flying. And now in just 48 hours, you can give a gift that will provide that warmth and love to those in need, whether it is for a family member or someone you may never meet,

And as we have always said, it doesn't have to be 48 hours at one time. It can be an hour for 48 days, or three hours for 16 days. Just don't watch the clock while you crochet these afghans, Enjoy the time you spend, and if it adds up to more or less than the magic 48, remember no one is counting!

Jean Leinhauser   *Rita Weiss*

Light and airy, this afghan uses an interesting cluster stitch that is fun to do and adds nice texture.

ROSEY OUTLOOK

SKILL LEVEL: INTERMEDIATE ⬛⬛⬛⬜

DESIGNED BY JEAN LEINHAUSER

SIZE

45" x 50" (114 cm x 127 cm)

MATERIALS

Medium weight yarn

[100% acrylic, 3.5 ounces, 170 yards (100 grams, 156 meters) per skein]

11 skeins dusty rose

Note: *Photographed model made with Lion Brand® Vanna's Choice® #140 Dusty Rose*

Size H (5mm) crochet hook (or size required for gauge)

GAUGE

7 dc = 2" (5 cm)

STITCH GUIDE

Cluster (CL): *YO, insert hook in specified place and draw up a lp to height of a dc; YO and draw through 2 lps; rep from * twice in same place; YO and draw through 4 lps.

V-stitch (V-st): Work (dc, ch 1, dc) in specified ch or sp.

INSTRUCTIONS

Ch 160.

Row 1 (right side): Dc in 6th ch from hook and in next 2 chs; work CL around 3-dc group just made (in sp between first dc made and turning ch); *skip 2 chs, V-st in next ch, skip 2 chs, dc in each of next 3 chs, work CL around 3-dc group just made (in sp between first dc of this group and last V-st); rep from * across to last 2 chs, skip next ch, dc in last ch; ch 3 (counts as a dc on following rows), turn.

Row 2: *Dc in top of CL and in each of next 3 dc, V-st in center ch-1 sp of next V-st; rep from * across, ending last rep with dc in last CL, dc in last 3 dc and in top of turning ch; ch 3 (counts as first dc of following row throughout pattern), turn.

Row 3: *Dc in next 3 dc, work CL as before, V-st in ch-1 sp of next V-st; rep from * across, ending last rep with dc in top of turning ch; ch 3, turn.

Repeat Rows 2 and 3 until piece measures about 50" (127 cm), ending by working a Row 2. Finish off.

EDGING

Hold piece with right side facing and last row worked at top. Join yarn with sc in first st at right, work 2 more sc in same st (corner made); sc evenly around all four sides of afghan, adjusting sts as needed to keep work flat, and working 3 sc in each outer corner st. Finish off. Weave in yarn ends.

FRINGE

Following Single Knot Fringe Instructions on page 40, cut yarn strands 13" long and using 5 strands in each knot, space knots evenly across each short end of afghan.

Made with soft and cuddly yarn, this cosy throw is just one great big granny square!
It's easy and quick to make with bulky yarn and a large hook.

QUICK GRANNY THROW

SKILL LEVEL: EASY ◖■□▭

DESIGNED BY LISA GENTRY

SIZE

45" x 45" (114 cm x 114 cm)

MATERIALS

Super Bulky weight yarn (6)

[100% acrylic, 6 ounces, 140 yards (170 grams, 128 meters)] per skein

   5 skeins green blend (A)

   2 skeins cream, tan blend (B)

Note: *Photographed model made with Red Heart® Light and Lofty® #9970 Green Gables (A) and Café au Lait (B)*

Size N (10 mm) crochet hook (or size required for gauge)

GAUGE

5 dc = 4" (10 cm)

4 rows = 4" (10 cm) in pattern st

INSTRUCTIONS

With Color A, ch 5, join with a sl st to form a ring.

Rnd 1: Ch 3 (counts as a dc), 2 dc in ring, ch 1; (3 dc in ring, ch 1) 3 times: 4 groups of 3 dc and 4 ch-1 sps; join with a sl st in top of beg ch-3.

Rnd 2: Sl st into next 2 dc and into ch-1 sp; in same sp work (ch 3, 2 dc, ch 1, 3 dc), ch 1; * (3 dc, ch 1, 3 dc) in next ch-1 sp, ch 1; rep from * around; join with a sl st in top of beg ch-3.

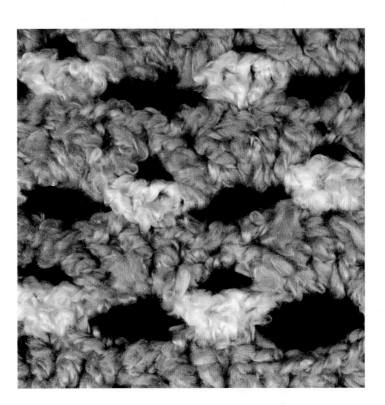

Rnd 3: Sl st in next 2 dc and into next ch-1 sp; ch 4 (counts as dc and ch-1 sp), 3 dc in same ch-1 sp; *ch 1, 3 dc in next ch-1 sp, ch 1, (3 dc, ch 1, 3 dc) in next ch-1 sp; rep from * twice more, ch 1, 3 dc in next ch-1 sp, ch 1, 2 dc in first ch-1 sp; join with a sl st in 3rd ch of beg ch-4, changing to Color B in last st.

Instructions continued on page 8

7

QUICK GRANNY THROW

Rnd 4: With Color B, sl st across to ch-1 sp, (sc, ch 1, 3 sc) in same sp for corner; *ch 1, 2 sc in next ch-1 sp, ch 3, 2 sc in next ch-1 sp, ch 1, (3 sc, ch 1, 3 sc) in next sp for corner; rep from * twice more; ch 1, 2 sc in next ch-1 sp, ch 3, 2 sc in next ch-1 sp, ch 1, 2 sc in first corner sp, join with a sl st in first sc, changing to Color A in last st.

Rnd 5: With Color A, sl st to corner sp, ch 4, 3 dc in same sp; *ch 1, 2 sc in next ch-1 sp, 5 dc in ch-3 sp, 2 sc in next ch-1 sp, ch 1; (3 dc, ch 1, 3 dc) in corner sp; rep from * twice more; ch 1, 2 sc in next ch-1 sp, 5 dc in ch-3 sp, 2 sc in next ch-1 sp, ch 1, 2 dc in first corner sp; sl st in 3rd ch of beginning ch-4, changing to Color B in last st.

Rnd 6: With Color B, sl st to corner sp, (sc, ch 1, 3 sc) in same sp; *ch 1, 2 sc in next ch-1 sp, ch 3, skip next 2 sc and 2 dc, work 3 sc in next dc, ch 3, skip next 2 dc and 2 sc, 2 sc in next ch-1 sp, ch 1; (3 sc, ch 1, 3 sc) in corner sp; rep from * twice more, ch 1, 2 sc in next ch-1 sp, ch 3, skip next 2 dc, work 3 sc in next dc, ch 3, skip next 2 dc and 2 sc, 2 sc in next ch-1 sp, ch 1, 2 sc in first corner sp, sl st in first sc, changing to Color A in last st.

Rnd 7: With Color A, sl st to first corner sp, ch 4, 3 dc in same sp; *ch 1, 2 sc in next ch-1 sp, work 5 dc in each ch-3 sp to next ch-1 sp, 2 sc in next ch-1 sp, ch 1; (3 dc, ch 1, 3 dc) in corner sp; rep from * twice more, ch 1, 2 sc in next ch-1 sp, work 5 dc in each ch-3 sp to next ch-1 sp, 2 sc in next ch-1 sp, ch 1, 2 dc in first corner sp; slip st in 3rd ch of beg ch-4, changing to Color B in last st.

Rnd 8: With Color B, sl st in next ch-1 sp, (sc, ch 1, 3 sc) in same sp; *ch 1, 2 sc in next ch-1 sp, ch 3; (skip next 4 sts, work 3 sc in next dc, ch 3) across to next ch-1 sp, 2 sc in next ch-1 sp, ch 1; (3 sc, ch 1, 3 sc) in corner sp; rep from * twice more, ch 1, 2 sc in next ch-1 sp, ch 3; (skip next 4 sts, work 3 sc in next dc, ch 3) across to next ch-1 sp, 2 sc in next ch-1 sp, ch 1, 2 sc in first corner sp, sl st in first sc, changing to Color A in last st.

Rnds 9 through 26: Rep Rnds 7 and 8 in sequence.

Rnd 27: With Color A, sl st to ch-1 sp, ch 4, 3 dc in same sp; *work 5 dc in each ch-1 sp and in each ch-3 sp across to next corner sp; work (3 dc, ch 1, 3 dc) in corner sp; rep from * twice more; work 5 dc in each ch-1 sp and ch-3 sp across to first corner sp, 2 dc in first corner sp; join with a sl st in 3rd ch of beg ch-4. Finish off; weave in all yarn ends.

Rich Tuscan colors, so popular in decorating today, are combined with textured stitches to create a bright and beautiful afghan.

A TOUCH OF TUSCANY

SKILL LEVEL: INTERMEDIATE ◖■■◻

DESIGNED BY JEAN LEINHAUSER

SIZE

Approximately 44" x 50" (112 cm 127 cm)

MATERIALS

Medium weight yarn

[100% acrylic, 16 ounces, 835 yards (438 grams, 763 meters) per skein]

　1 skein lt sage (A)

[100% acrylic, 7 ounces, 364 yards (198 grams, 333 meters) per skein]

　1 skein carrot (B)

　1 skein burgundy (C)

　1 skein gold (D)

　1 skein café (E)

　1 skein blue (F)

Note: *Photographed model made with Red Heart® Super Saver® #631 Light Sage (A), #0256 Carrot (B); #0376 Burgundy (C); #0321 Gold (D); #0360 Café (E) and #0886 Blue (F)*

Size I (5.5 mm) crochet hook (or size required for gauge)

GAUGE

12 dc = 4" (10 cm)

STITCH GUIDE

Back Popcorn (bPC): Work 5 dc in specified st; drop lp from hook, insert hook from back to front in top of first dc made, pick up dropped lp and draw through lp on hook. Popcorn will appear on the reverse side of the work.

Single crochet decrease (sc dec): (Draw up a lp in next st) twice, YO and draw through all 3 lps on hook.

Instructions continued on page 11

A Touch of Tuscany

INSTRUCTIONS

With Color A, ch 134.

Row 1: Dc in 4th ch from hook and in each rem ch: 132 dc; ch 3 (counts as first dc of following row here and throughout), turn.

Row 2: Dc in next dc, dc in each remaining dc across; ch 3, turn.

Row 3: Rep Row 2, changing to Color B in last st; with Color B, ch 3, turn.

Row 4: Continuing with Color B, *skip next dc, dc in next dc; working in front of dc just made, dc in skipped st; rep from * across, ending dc in top of turning ch-3; ch 3, turn.

Rows 5: Rep Row 4, changing to Color C in last st; with Color C, ch 3, turn.

Rows 6 and 7: Continuing with Color C, dc in next st and in each rem st across, changing to Color D in last st of Row 7; ch 1, turn.

Row 8: Continuing with Color D, sc in first 65 dc, sc dec over next 2 sts, sc in each rem dc: 131 sc; ch 3, turn.

Row 9: Dc in next sc; *PC in next sc, dc in each of next 2 sc; rep from * across; ch 1, turn.

Row 10: Sc in first 65 sts, 2 sc in next dc; sc in each rem st across, changing to Color E in last st: 132 sc; with Color E, ch 3, turn.

Row 11: Continuing with Color E, skip next st, dc in next st; working in front of dc just made, dc in skipped st; ch 3, turn.

Rows 12 and 13: Rep Row 11, changing to Color F in last st of Row 13; with color F, ch 1, turn.

Rows 14 through 16: Continuing with Color F, sc in each st across; at end of Row 16, change to Color A in last st; ch 3, turn.

Rows 17 through 19: Continuing with Color A, dc in next st and in each rem st across, changing to Color B in last st of Row 19; with color B, ch 3, turn.

Rep Rows 4 through 19 until piece measures about 50" (127 cm) long, ending by working a Row 19. At end of last row, do not ch or turn. Finish off; weave in all yarn ends.

FRINGE

Following Single Knot Fringe instructions on page 40, using all colors of leftover yarn, cut yarn strands 16" (40.64 cm) long for fringe. Using 4 strands of a variety of colors in each knot, tie knots spaced about 2 sts apart across each short end of afghan. Trim fringe as desired.

A pretty peach center accented with a whipped cream border
is easy to make and a delight to use.

PEACH SUNDAE CUDDLER

SKILL LEVEL: EASY ◖■□□

DESIGNED BY MARY JANE PROTUS

SIZE

36" x 36" (91.5 cm x 91.5 cm)

MATERIALS

Super bulky weight yarn

[100% acrylic, 6 ounces, 140 yards (127 grams, 128 meters) per skein]

4 skeins peach (A)

2 ounces white (B)

Note: *Photographed model made with Red Heart® Baby Clouds™ #9322 Creamsicle (A) and #9311 Cloud*

Size 15 (10 mm) crochet hook (or size required for gauge)

GAUGE

7 sts = 3" (7.62 cm) in pattern st

7 rows = 3" (7.6 cm)

INSTRUCTIONS

With A, ch 84.

Row 1 (right side): Sc in 2nd ch from hook; *ch 1, skip next ch, sc in next ch: rep from * across; turn.

Row 2: Ch 1, sc in first sc; *ch 1, skip ch-1 sp, sc in next sc; rep from * across; turn.

Rep Row 2 until piece measures 36" (91.5 cm) from beg ch. Finish off; weave in yarn ends.

EDGING

With right side facing, join B at top right corner in first sc; working around entire outer edge of afghan, ch 1, (sc, ch 1, sc) in first sc; *ch 1, skip next ch-1 sp, sc in next sc; rep from * around, working (sc, ch 1, sc) in each remaining outer corner st. Join with a sl st in first sc. Finish off; weave in yarn ends.

Lovely pastel stripes are formed by the yarn used in the photographed model. If you choose another yarn, you can alternate colors to get the same stripe affect. A perky ruffle completes this special creation for a favorite baby.

SWEET BABY

SKILL LEVEL: EASY ◨■☐☐

DESIGNED BY JEAN LEINHAUSER

SIZE

40" x 40" (102 cm x 102 cm) before ruffles

MATERIALS

Medium weight yarn 〔④〕

[100% acrylic, 3.5 ounces, 278 yards (100 grams, 254 meters) per ball]

8 balls

Note: *Photographed model made with Red Heart® Sweet Baby™ # 7788 Dream Girl*

Size I (5.5 mm) crochet hook (or size required for gauge)

GAUGE

16 sc = 4" (10 cm)

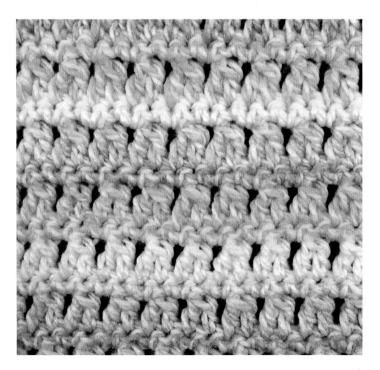

STITCH GUIDE

Cluster (Cl): (YO, insert hook in next st and draw up a lp, YO and draw through first 2 lps on hook) twice, YO and draw through all 3 lps on hook.

INSTRUCTIONS

Ch 161.

Foundation Row: Sc in 2nd ch from hook and in each rem ch: 160 sc; ch 3 (counts as first dc of following row here and throughout pattern), turn.

Pattern Row 1: *Work Cl over next 2 sts, ch 1; rep from * across, ending with dc in last st; ch 1, turn.

Pattern Row 2: Sc in first dc, *sc in top of next Cl, sc in next ch-1 sp; rep from * across, ending with sc in top of turning ch; ch 3, turn.

Rep Pattern Rows 1 and 2 alternately until piece measures about 40" (101.6 cm) long, ending by working a Row 2. Finish off; weave in all yarn ends.

RUFFLED BORDER

Hold afghan with last row at top.

Rnd 1: Join yarn with a sl st in first st at right corner, ch 1, work 3 sc for corner in same st; sc in each st across to next corner, work 3 sc in corner; working now across long side of afghan, sc across, adjusting sts to keep work flat, to next corner; work 3 sc in corner; sc in unused lps of starting ch to corner, work 3 sc in corner; sc across last side, adjusting sts to keep work flat, join with a sl st in beg sc.

Rnd 2: Sl st into next sc; ch 3, dc in same sc; *3 dc in next sc, 2 sc in next sc; rep from * around, join with a sc in top of beg ch-3.

Rnd 3: *Ch 3, skip next st, sc in next st; rep from * around; join with a sl st in beg sc.

Finish off; weave in all yarn ends.

A super bulky weight yarn works up quickly and creates a soft and warm afghan perfect for those chilly evenings.

WARM AND CUDDLY AFGHAN

SKILL LEVEL: INTERMEDIATE ◼◼◼◻

DESIGNED BY GLENDA WINKLEMAN

SIZE

40" x 64" (101.5 cm x 162.5 cm)

MATERIALS

Super bulky weight yarn

[100% acrylic, 6 ounces, 140 yards (170 grams, 128 meters) 33 per skein]

   3 skeins brown multi (A)

   8 skeins cream (B)

Note: *Photographed model made with Red Heart® Light and Lofty® #9617 Pheasant (A) and #9334 Café au Lait (B)*

Size P (11.5 mm) crochet hook (or size required for gauge)

Yarn or tapestry needle with large eye for weaving

GAUGE

7 sts = 3" (7.6 cm) in pattern

5 rows = 5" (12.7 cm) in pattern

STITCH GUIDE

Sc-picot: Sc, ch 3, sl st in sc just made

INSTRUCTIONS

With Color B, ch 92.

Row 1 (right side): Sc in 2nd ch from hook; * ch 1, skip next ch, sc in next ch; rep from * across: 46 sc; ch 1, turn.

Row 2: Sc in first sc, sc in next ch-1 sp; * ch 1, skip next sc, sc in next ch-1 sp; rep from *across to last 2 sts, sc in next ch-1 sp, sc in last sc; ch 1, turn.

Instructions continued on page 18

WARM AND CUDDLY AFGHAN

Row 3: Sc in first sc; * ch 1, skip next sc, sc in next ch-1 sp; rep from * across to last 2 sc, ch 1, skip next sc, sc in last sc; ch 1, turn.

Rep Rows 2 and 3 until piece measures about 64" (162.5 cm) long. At end of last row, do not turn, finish off. Weave in yarn ends.

WEAVING

With right side of afghan facing you, use a yarn needle to start weaving the first row as follows:

First woven row: Thread 2 strands of Color A into yarn needle. Leaving several inches of yarn hanging at edge, bring needle up from back through first ch-1 sp, *insert needle down in next ch-1 sp, bring needle up in next ch-1 sp**; rep from * to ** across. Knot end to last st; weave in end. At opposite side, knot yarn end to edge and weave in end.

Skip next row (Row 2).

Second woven row: Thread 2 strands of Color A into yarn needle. Working in Row 3, bring yarn down from front of work through first ch-1 sp, leaving a yarn end at edge; bring needle up in next ch-1 sp, then down in following sp; continue to weave up and down across row. Knot yarn ends to edge as before and weave in ends.

Skip next row (Row 4).

Working in the next row (Row 5), continue to weave 2 strands of A in this manner, weaving in every other row of afghan and alternating the first and second woven rows.

AFGHAN BORDER

With right side of afghan facing, join Color B in top right hand corner sc.

Rnd 1: *Ch 1, sc in first sc; work (ch 1, skip next ch-1 sp, sc in next sc) across edge to next corner; ch 1, working side edge, skip first row, sc in end st of next row; then work (ch 1, skip next row, sc in end st of next row) along length to corner**, working across bottom, rep from * to **; ch 1, join with sl st to beg sc.

Rnd 2: Sl st in ch-1 sp, ch 1; *sc-picot in next sc, sc in next ch 1-sp; rep from * around; join with sl st in sc of beg sc-picot. Finish off; weave in yarn ends.

*This lacy afghan, created with stacked shells, is truly elegant.
Choose any solid color to accent a color scheme.*

SHELL ON SHELL

SKILL LEVEL: INTERMEDIATE ⬛⬛⬛⬜

DESIGNED BY JEAN LEINHAUSER

SIZE

45" x 52" (114 cm x 132 cm)

MATERIALS

Worsted weight yarn

[100% acrylic, 6 ounces, 315 yards (171 grams, 218 meters) per skein]

7 skeins blue

Note: *Photographed model made with Caron® Simply Soft® #9709 Light Country Blue*

Size I (5.5mm) crochet hook (or size required for gauge)

GAUGE

14 sc = 4" (10 cm)

STITCH GUIDE

Cluster (CL): *YO, insert hook in specified st and draw up a lp to height of a dc, YO and draw through 2 lps; rep from * once more, YO and draw through 3 lps.

Cluster Shell (CLS): In specified st work (3 dc, CL, 3 dc).

INSTRUCTIONS

Ch 162.

Row 1: Sc in 2nd ch from hook and in each rem ch; ch 1, turn.

Row 2: Sc in first 3 sc; *skip 2 sc, CLS in next sc, skip 2 sc, sc in each of next 5 sc; rep from * across, ending last rep with sc in last 3 (instead of 5) sc; ch 1, turn.

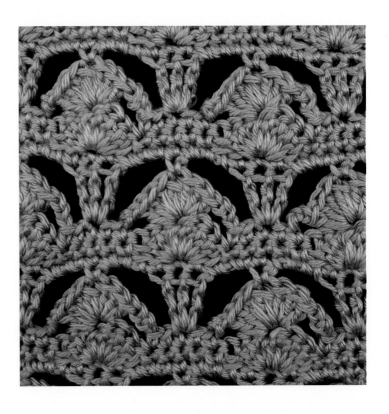

Instructions continued on page 21

19

SHELL ON SHELL

Row 3 (right side): Sc in first 3 sc; * ch 3, CLS in top of next CL, ch 3, sc in next 5 sc; rep from * across, ending last rep with sc in last 3 (instead of 5) sc; ch 4 (counts as a tr on following row), turn.

Row 4: Tr in base of turning ch; *ch 3, sc in top of next CL, ch 3, skip next 2 sc, 3 tr in next sc; rep from * across, ending last rep with 2 tr (instead of 3) in last sc; ch 1, turn.

Row 5: Sc in each of first 2 tr; *3 sc in ch-3 sp, sc in next sc, 3 sc in next ch-3 sp, sc in each of next 3 tr; rep from * across, ending last rep with sc in last tr and in top of turning ch; ch 3 (counts as a dc on following row), turn.

Row 6: Work 3 dc in base of turning ch, skip next 2 sc, sc in next 5 sc; * skip 2 sc, CLS in next sc, skip 2 sc, sc in next 5 sc; rep from * across, ending last rep with skip 2 sc, 4 dc in last sc; ch 3, turn.

Row 7: Work 3 dc in base of turning ch, ch 3, sc in next 5 sc; *ch 3, CLS in top of next CL, ch 3, sc in next 5 sc; rep from * across, ending last rep with ch 3, 4 dc in top of turning ch; ch 1, turn.

Row 8: Sc in first dc; *ch 3, skip 2 sc, 3 tr in next sc, ch 3, **sc in next CL; rep from * across, ending last rep at **; sc in top of turning ch; ch 1, turn.

Row 9: Sc in first sc; *3 sc in ch-3 sp, sc in each of next 3 tr, 3 sc in next ch-3 sp, **sc in next sc; rep from * across, ending last rep at **; sc in last sc; ch 1, turn.

Rep Rows 2 through 9 until piece measures about 52" (132 cm), ending by working a Row 9.

Finish off; weave in yarn ends.

SIDE EDGINGS

First Side

Hold piece with wrong side facing and one long edge at top.

Row 1: Join yarn in first st at right. Sc evenly across sides of rows, adjusting sts as needed to keep work flat. At end, ch 1, turn.

Row 2: Sc in each sc, adjusting sts as needed to keep work flat. Finish off; weave in yarn ends.

Second Side

On opposite long edge, work as for First Side.

The all-time favorite wave pattern here blends two colors, with crisp white topping the gently undulating rows formed with easy double crochet stitches.

CRESTED WAVE AFGHAN

SKILL LEVEL: INTERMEDIATE ⬛⬛⬛◻

DESIGNED BY MICHELE THOMPSON

SIZE

50" x 61" (127 cm x 155 cm)

MATERIALS

Super bulky weight yarn

[100% acrylic, 6 ounces, 140 yards (170 grams, 128 meters) per skein]

    26 ounces cream (A)

    22 ounces white (B)

Note: *Photographed model was made with Red Heart® "Light & Lofty® # 9334 Café Au Lait (Color A) and #9316 Puff (Color B).*

Size P (11.5 mm) crochet hook or size required for gauge

GAUGE

19 sts = 10" (25 cm) in pattern

10 rows = 10" (25 cm) in pattern

STITCH GUIDE

Double Crochet Decrease (dc dec): *YO, insert hook in next sc, YO and draw up a lp; YO and draw through 2 lps on hook; rep from * once more, YO and draw through all 3 lps on hook.

Note: *Each dc dec is worked over 2 sts.*

Changing Colors in Single Crochet: With color in use, draw up a lp in last st, drop this color, pick up new color and draw through 2 lps on hook. Cut first color; continue with new color.

Back Loops: The back lp of a stitch is the loop away from you.

Instructions continued on page 24

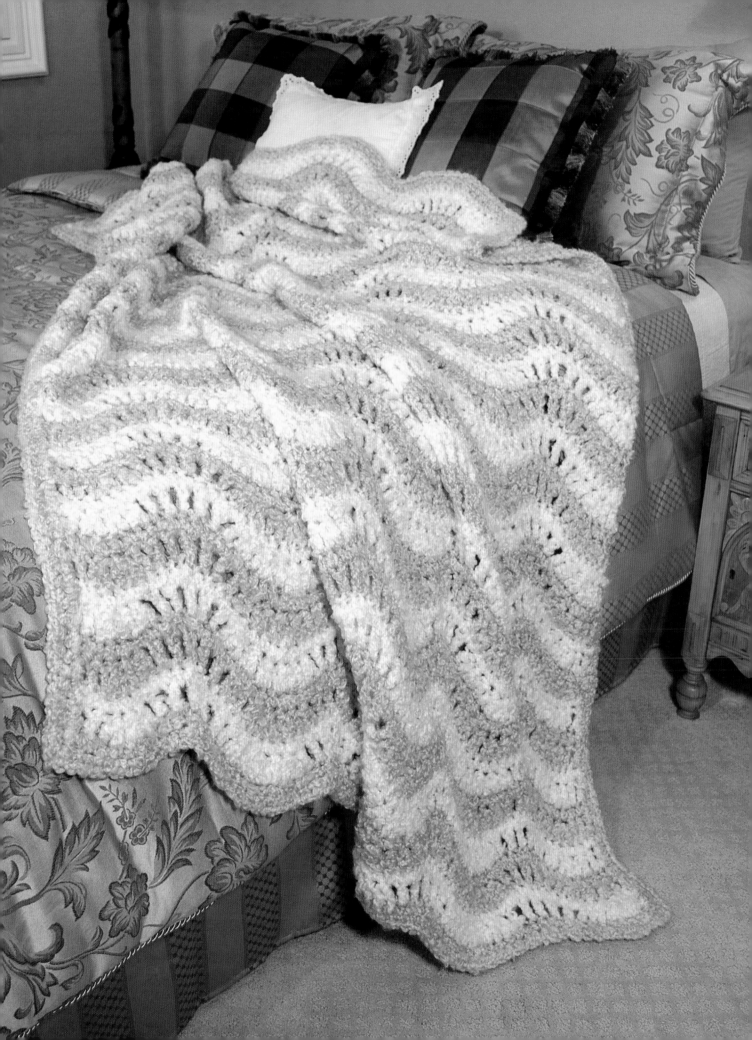

CRESTED WAVE AFGHAN

INSTRUCTIONS

With Color A, ch 95.

Row 1 (wrong side): Sc in 2nd ch from hook and in each ch across, changing to Color B in last st: 94 sc; turn.

Row 2 (right side): With Color B, ch 3 (counts as first dc), skip first sc, working in back lps only of each st, dc in next sc, work dc dec 3 times; * (ch 1, dc in next sc) 6 times **, work dc dec 6 times; rep from * to last 8 sc, end last rep at **; work dc dec 3 times, dc in last 2 sc: 5 waves made; turn.

Row 3: Ch 1, working now in both lps of each st, sc in first 6 sts, *(sc in ch-1 sp, sc in next st) 6 times **, sc in next 6 sts; rep from * to last 4 sts, ending last rep at **; sc in next 3 sts, sc in top of ch-3, changing to Color A in last st; turn.

Rep Rows 2 and 3 for pattern, working 2 rows Color A and 2 rows Color B alternately until piece measures about 59" from beg. Finish off; weave in all yarn ends.

EDGING

Row 1 (right side): With right side facing, join Color A at bottom right hand corner; ch 1, sc evenly up right side edge, work 3 sc in corner, sc across top, work 3 sc in next corner, sc evenly down left side edge; turn.

Rnd 2: Ch 1, sc evenly around, working 3 sc in corners and working sc across unused lps of bottom chain edge; join with a sl st in first sc. Finish off; weave in yarn ends.

When young Victorian ladies carried their fans, they were designed not only to provide a breath of cool air but to flirt with the eligible bachelors lined up for their inspection. Fan flirting has passed into history, but these pretty little crocheted fans add a romantic touch to this afghan.

FLIRTY FANS

SKILL LEVEL: INTERMEDIATE ⬤◼◼◻▭

DESIGNED BY JEAN LEINHAUSER

SIZE

46" x 52" (117 cm x 132 cm)

MATERIALS

Medium weight yarn

[100% acrylic, 7 ounces, 366 yards (198 grams, 334.7 meters) per skein]

   7 skeins orchid

Note: *Photographed model made with Caron® Simply Soft® # 9717 Orchid*

Size H (5mm) crochet hook (or size required for gauge)

GAUGE

2 Fans = 4" (10 cm)

STITCH GUIDE

Fan: In specified st work (dc, ch 1) 4 times, dc in same st.

Back post double crochet (BPdc): YO, insert hook from back to front to back around post (vertical bar) of specified st; YO and draw up a lp to height of a dc; (YO and draw through 2 lps) twice.

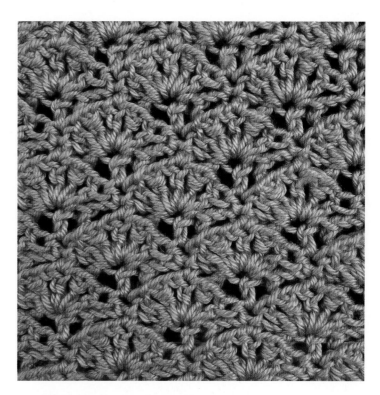

INSTRUCTIONS

Ch 234.

Row 1 (wrong side): Sc in 2nd ch from hook; *skip 3 chs, work Fan in next ch, **skip 3 chs, sc in next ch; rep from * across, ending last rep at **; skip 3 chs, sc in last ch; ch 3 (counts as a dc on following row), turn.

Row 2: *BPdc around 2nd dc of next fan, ch 2, sc in next dc, ch 2, BPdc around next dc, dc in next sc; rep from * across; ch 4 (counts as a dc and ch-1 sp), turn.

Instructions continued on page 27

FLIRTY FANS

Row 3: (Dc, ch 1, dc) in base of ch; *sc in next sc, work Fan in next dc; rep from * across to last sc, sc in last sc, in top of turning ch work (dc, ch 1) twice, dc in same place; ch 1, turn.

Row 4: Sc in first dc, ch 2, BPdc around next dc; dc in next sc; *BPdc around 2nd dc of next Fan, ch 2, sc in next dc, ch 2, BPdc around next dc, dc in next sc; rep from * across, ending last rep with BPdc around last dc, ch 2, sc in top of turning ch; ch 1, turn.

Row 5: Sc in first sc; *work Fan in next dc, sc in next sc; rep from * across; ch 3, turn.

Rep Rows 2 through 5 until piece measures about 52" (132 cm), ending by working a Row 5. Finish off.

BOTTOM BORDER

Hold afghan with wrong side facing and foundation ch at top. Working in unused lps of foundation ch, join yarn with sc in first ch at right; *skip 3 chs, work Fan in next ch (same ch in which Fan of Row 1 was previously worked), skip 3 chs, sc in next ch; rep from * across. Finish off.

SIDE EDGINGS

First Side
Row 1: Hold afghan with wrong side facing and one long edge at top. Join yarn with sc in first row at right; working in sides of rows, sc evenly along edge, adjusting sts as needed to keep work flat; ch 1, turn.

Row 2: Sc in each sc across, again adjusting sts as needed to keep work flat. Finish off; weave in yarn ends.

Second Side
Row 1: Hold afghan with wrong side facing and opposite long edge at top. Work as for First Side.

Soft as a summer cloud, this blue and white throw is worked with long stitches, adding an interesting texture and dimension.

CLOUDS BY THE SEASIDE THROW

SKILL LEVEL: EASY ◖■□□▭

DESIGNED BY MARY JANE PROTUS

SIZE

36" (91.5 cm) x 45" (114 cm)

MATERIALS

Super bulky weight yarn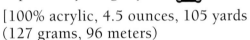

[100% acrylic, 4.5 ounces, 105 yards (127 grams, 96 meters)

4 skeins multicolor (A)

[100% acrylic, 6 ounces, 140 yards (170 grams, 128 meters) per skein]

3 skeins white (B)

Note: *Photographed model made with Red Heart® Baby Clouds™ #9975 (A) Seashore and #9311 Cloud (B)*

Size N (10 mm) crochet hook (or size required for gauge

Yarn needle

GAUGE

8 sts = 4" (10 cm) in pattern

6 rows = 4" (10 cm) in pattern

STITCH GUIDE

Long double crochet (Ldc): YO and draw up a lp in unworked sc 3 rows below; (YO and draw through 2 lps on hook) twice.

To change color in single crochet: Draw up a lp in last st before color change, drop first color; with new color YO and draw through 2 lps on hook; cut first color and continue with new color.

Instructions continued on page 30

CLOUDS BY THE SEASIDE THROW

INSTRUCTIONS

With A, ch 72.

Row 1: Sc in 2nd ch from hook and in each rem ch across, changing to B in last sc: 71 sc; ch 3, turn.

Row 2 (right side): Continuing with B, skip first sc, dc in next 2 sc; *ch 1, skip next sc, dc in next 3 sc; rep from* across; ch 1, turn.

Row 3: Sc in first 3 sts; *ch 1, skip ch-1 sp, sc in next 3 sts; rep from * across, working last sc in top of ch-3 and changing to A in last st; ch 4, turn.

Row 4: Continuing with A, skip first 2 sc, dc in next sc; *work Ldc in free sc 3 rows below enclosing Rows 2 and 3 within st, dc in next sc, ch 1, skip next sc, dc in next sc; rep from * across; ch 1, turn.

Row 5: Sc in first dc, ch 1, skip next ch-1 sp; *sc in next 3 sts, ch 1, skip next ch-1 sp; rep from * to last st; sc in 3rd ch of ch- 4, changing to B in last st; ch 3, turn.

Row 6: Skip first sc, work Ldc, in free sc 3 rows below, dc in next sc; *ch 1, skip next sc, dc in next sc, work Ldc in free sc 3 rows below; dc in next sc; rep from * across; ch 1, turn.

Rep Rows 3 through 6 in sequence until piece measures about 44" (112 cm) from beg, ending by working a Row 3.

Last Row: Continuing with A, sc in first 3 sts; *work Ldc in free sc 3 rows below, sc in next 3 sts; rep from * across. Finish off; weave in yarn ends.

EDGING

With right side of work facing you, join A with a sl st in top right corner, ch 1; * work (sc, ch 1, sc) in corner; sc evenly along next edge to next corner; rep from * around; join with a sl st in beg sc. Finish off; weave in yarn ends.

This rythmic cluster stitch, easy and quick to do, provides a nice texture to the solid color afghan.

CLEVER CLUSTERS

SKILL LEVEL: INTERMEDIATE

DESIGNED BY JEAN LEINHAUSER

SIZE

45" x 50" (114 cm x 127 cm)

MATERIALS

Medium weight yarn

[100% acrylic, 3.5 ounces, 170 yards (100 grams, 156 meters) per skein]

   12 skeins pink

Note: *Photographed model made with Lion Brand® Vanna's Choice® #142 Rose*

Size I (5.5 mm) crochet hook (or size required for gauge)

GAUGE

6 Clusters = 4" (10 cm)

STITCH GUIDE

Cluster (CL): YO, insert hook in specified st and draw up a lp to height of a dc; YO and draw through 2 lps; (YO, insert hook in same st and draw up a lp to same height, YO and draw through 2 lps) twice; YO and draw through 4 lps; ch 1.

Instructions continued on page 33

CLEVER CLUSTERS

INSTRUCTIONS

Ch 148.

Row 1: Sc in 2nd ch from hook and in next ch; *ch 1, skip next ch, sc in next ch; rep from * across to last 3 chs, ch 1, skip next ch, sc in last 2 chs; ch 4 (counts as a dc and ch-1 sp on following row), turn.

Row 2 (right side): *Skip next sc, CL in next ch-1 sp, ch 1; rep from * across to last ch-1 sp, CL in last ch-1 sp, ch 1, skip next sc, dc in last sc; ch 1, turn.

Row 3: Sc in first dc, sc in first ch-1 sp; *ch 1, skip next CL, sc in next ch-1 sp; rep from * across, ending last rep with sc in turning ch sp, sc in 3rd ch of turning ch; ch 4, turn.

Repeat Rows 2 and 3 until piece measures about 50" (127 cm). Finish off.

BORDER

Hold piece with right side facing and last row worked at top; join yarn with sc in first st at right; in same st work 2 more sc for corner; work sc evenly around entire afghan, adjusting sts as needed to keep work flat, and working 3 sc in one st at each corner. Finish off; weave in yarn ends.

FRINGE

Following Single Knot Fringe instructions on page 40, cut fringe 13" long. Using one piece of yarn in each knot, tie a knot in each sc across each short end of afghan. Trim evenly if desired.

Bright and as much fun as a box of crayons, this child's afghan can also do double duty as a play rug. The beloved Log Cabin design is worked in a join-as-you-go method that eliminates sewing motifs together.

CRAYON BOX
JOIN-AS-YOU-GO LOG CABIN

SKILL LEVEL: INTERMEDIATE ●■■◻

DESIGNED BY MARTY MILLER

SIZE

53½" x 58" (136 cm x 147 cm)

MATERIALS

Medium weight yarn

[100% acrylic, 5 ounces, 290 yards (140 grams, 265 meters) per skein]

   1 skein lt blue (A)

   1 skein pink (B)

   1 skein yellow (C)

   1 skein lime (D)

   1 skein orange (E)

   1 skein dk blue (F)

   2 skeins red (G)

[100% acrylic, 7 ounces, 364 yards (198 grams, 333 meters) per skein]

   1 skein white (H)

Note: *Photographed model made with Red Heart® Kids™ #2846 Cruise Blue (A), #2734 Pink (B), #2230 Yellow (C), #2652 Lime (D), #2252 Orange (E), #2845 Blue (F), #2390 Red (G) and Red Heart® Super Saver® #0311 White (H)*

   Size I (5.5 mm) crochet hook (or size required for gauge)

GAUGE

First 3 rnds = 4.5" square

STITCH GUIDE

Foundation double crochet eyelet (Fdc eyelet): *Ch 3, dc in 3rd ch from hook (this ch-3 is the "eyelet"); rep from * for as many Fdc eyelets as needed.

PATTERN NOTES

1. All squares and rectangles are worked on the right side. Do not turn at the end of a round.

2. The ch-3 at the beginning of each round counts as a dc.

Instructions continued on page 36

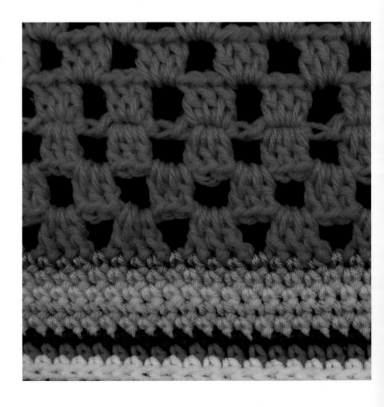

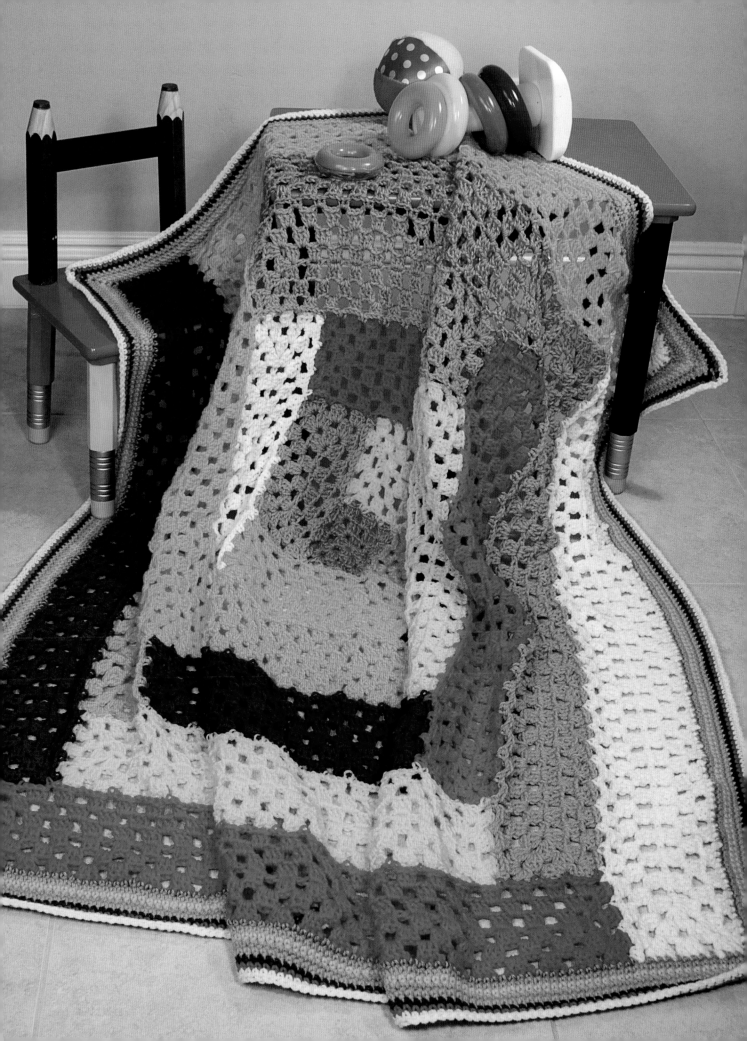

CRAYON BOX

INSTRUCTIONS

JOIN AS YOU GO INSTRUCTIONS

After Granny Square 1, join the last rnd of the next Granny Square and the last rnd of all following Granny Rectangles to the indicated rectangle or square already finished. Join while you are working on the side of the square or rectangle opposite from where you started. Instead of ch-2 between the shells, work 2 sc in the ch-2 space of the adjacent side of the finished square or rectangle. If you are attaching to 2 adjacent corners, work an sc in each adjacent corner.

Granny Square

Ch 4, join with a sl st in first ch to form a ring.

Rnd 1 (right side): Ch 3 (counts as dc here and throughout), 2 dc in ring, ch 2; (3 dc in ring, ch 2) 3 times; join with a sl st in 3rd ch of beg ch-3; sl st in each of next 2 dc and in next ch-2 sp: 12 dc and 4 ch-2 sps.

Rnd 2: Ch 3, in same ch-2 sp work (2 dc, ch 2, 3 dc): beg corner made; ch 2, *(3 dc, ch 2, 3 dc) in next ch-2 sp (corner made), ch 2; rep from * 2 more times; join with a sl st in 3rd ch of beg ch-3; sl st in each of next 2 dc and into next ch-2 sp: 24 dc and 8 ch-2 sps.

Rnd 3: (Ch 3, 2 dc, ch 2, 3 dc) in same ch-2 sp, ch 2, 3 dc in next ch-2 sp, ch 2; *(3 dc, ch 2, 3 dc) in next corner ch-2 sp, ch 2, 3 dc in next ch-2 sp, ch 2; rep from * 2 more times; join with sl st in 3rd ch of beg ch-3. Finish off; weave in yarn ends.

Granny Rectangle

Work 4 Fdc eyelets (see Stitch Guide).

Rnd 1: Ch 3, (2 dc, ch 2, 3 dc) in first eyelet sp (beg corner made), ch 2; (3 dc, ch 2) in each eyelet space to last eyelet sp, in last eyelet sp work (3 dc, ch 2) 3 times; working now on opposite side of the eyelets and skipping the last eyelet sp you worked in, (3dc, ch 2) in the next eyelet sp, and (3 dc, ch 2) in each eyelet sp to the last eyelet sp; in last eyelet sp work (3 dc, ch 2); join with a sl st in top of beg ch-3; sl st in each of next 2 dc and into next ch-2 sp at corner.

Rnd 2: In same corner sp, work (ch 3, 2 dc, 3 dc), *ch 2, work (3 dc, ch 2, 3 dc) in next corner sp, work (ch 2, 3 dc) in each ch-2 sp to next corner**, work (3 dc, ch 2, 3 dc) in next corner; rep from * to ** once; sl st in next 2 dc and into ch-2 sp.

Rnd 3: (Ch 3, 2 dc, ch 2, 3 dc) in same corner ch-2 sp, *ch 2, 3 dc in next sp; work (ch 2, 3 dc) twice in next corner; work (ch 2, 3 dc) in each sp to next corner**, (ch 2, 3 dc) twice in corner sp; rep from * to **. Join with sl st in top of ch-3. Finish off; weave in yarn ends.

Afghan Instructions

Following the schematic below, work squares and rectangles as follows:

Square #1 in Color A.

Square #2 in Color B, joining last rnd of Square 2 to Square 1, as above.

Rectangle #3 in Color C, starting with 4 Fdc eyelets, joining last rnd of 3 to 1 and 2.

Rectangle #4 in Color D, starting with 4 Fdc eyelets, joining last rnd of 4 to 1 and 3.

Rectangle #5 in Color E, starting with 7 Fdc eyelets, following the schematic for joining.

Rectangle #6 in Color F, starting with 7 Fdc eyelets, following the schematic for joining.

Rectangle #7 in Color G, starting with 10 Fdc eyelets, following the schematic for joining.

Rectangle #8 in Color H, starting with 10 Fdc eyelets, following the schematic for joining.

Rectangle #9 in Color B, starting with 13 Fdc eyelets, following the schematic for joining.

Rectangle #10 in Color C, starting with 13 Fdc eyelets, following the schematic for joining.

Rectangle #11 in Color D, starting with 16 Fdc eyelets, following the schematic for joining.

Rectangle #12 in Color E, starting with 16 Fdc eyelets, following the schematic for joining.

Rectangle #13 in Color F, starting with 19 Fdc eyelets, following the schematic for joining.

Rectangle #14 in Color G, starting with 19 Fdc eyelets, following the schematic for joining.

Rectangle #15 in Color A, starting with 22 Fdc eyelets, following the schematic for joining.

Instructions continued on page 38

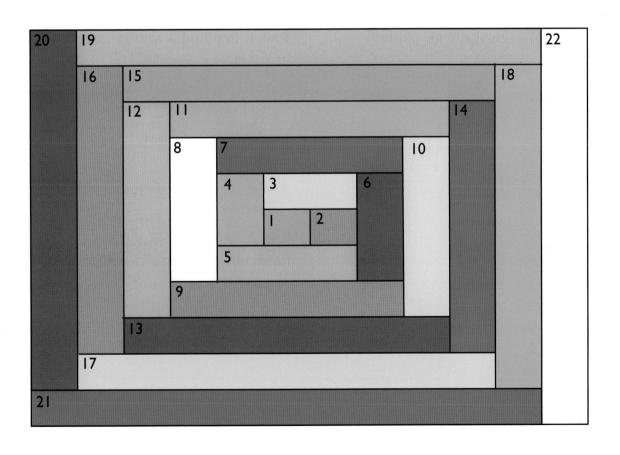

CRAYON BOX

Rectangle #16 in Color B, starting with 22 Fdc eyelets, following the schematic for joining.

Rectangle #17 in Color C, starting with 25 Fdc eyelets, following the schematic for joining.

Rectangle #18 in Color D, starting with 25 Fdc eyelets, following the schematic for joining.

Rectangle #19 in Color E, starting with 28 Fdc eyelets, following the schematic for joining.

Rectangle #20 in Color F, starting with 28 Fdc eyelets, following the schematic for joining.

Rectangle #21 in Color G, starting with 31 Fdc eyelets, following the schematic for joining.

Rectangle #22 in Color H, starting with 31 Fdc eyelets, following the schematic for joining.

Border

With right side facing, join Color A in 2nd dc before any ch-2 corner sp of a corner on last rnd.

Rnd 1: With Color A, ch 1, sc in each dc to ch-2 corner sp, work (sc, ch 3, sc) in same sp; *sc evenly along side, working 2 sc in each ch-2 sp; when you come to 2 adjacent corners of the rectangles, work 1 sc in each corner sp; continue to next corner of the afghan; (sc, ch-3, sc) in corner ch-2 sp; rep from * around, ending with sl st in first sc; change to Color B in last st; finish off Color A.

Rnd 2: With Color B, sc in each sc around, working (sc, ch 3, sc) in each corner ch-3 space; join with sl st in first sc changing to Color C in last st; finish off Color B.

Rnd 3: With Color C, rep Rnd 2; at end of rnd, change to Color D.

Rnd 4: Rep Rnd 2 with D, changing to Color E in last st.

Rnd 5: Rep Rnd 2 with Color E, changing to Color F in last st.

Rnd 6: Rep Rnd 2 with Color F, changing to Color G in last st.

Rnd 7: Rep Rnd 2 with Color G, changing to color H in last st.

Rnd 8: Rep Rnd 2 with Color H; at end of rnd, finish off; weave in all yarn ends.

GENERAL DIRECTIONS

ABBREVIATIONS AND SYMBOLS

Crochet patterns are written in a special shorthand which is used so that instructions don't take up too much space. They sometimes seem confusing, but once you learn them, you'll have no trouble following them.

These are Abbreviations

Beg	beginning
BL	back loop
BLO	back loop only
Cl(s)	cluster(s)
Ch(s)	chain(s)
Cm	centimeter
Cont	continue
Dc	double crochet
Dc dec	double crochet decrease
Dec	decrease
Ehdc	extended half double crochet
Esc	extended single crochet
Fig	figure
FPdc	front post double crochet
FPdtr	front post double triple crochet
FPtr	front post triple crochet
Hdc	half double crochet
Inc	increase(ing)
Long sc	long single croche
Lp(s)	loop(s)
Lp St	loop stitch
LscCl	long single crochet cluster
Mm	millimeter
Oz	ounce
Patt	pattern
PC	popcorn
Prev	previous
Pst	puff stitch
Rem	remaining
Rep	repeat(ing)
Rev	reverse
Rev sc	reverse single crochet
Rnd(s)	round(s)
Sc	single crochet
Sc2tog	single crochet decrease
Sl st	slip stitch
Sp(s)	space(s)
St(s)	stitch(es)
Tog	together
Tr	triple crochet
V-st	V-stitch
X-st	cross stitch
YO	yarn over hook

These are Standard Symbols

* An asterisk (or double asterisks**) in a pattern row, indicates a portion of instructions to be used more than once. For instance, "   rep from * three times" means that after working the instructions once, you must work them again three times for a total of 4 times in all.

† A dagger (or double daggers ††) indicates that those instructions will be repeated again later in the same row or round.

: The number of stitches after a colon tells you the number of stitches you will have when you have completed the row or round.

( ) Parentheses enclose instructions which are to be worked the number of times following the parentheses. For instance, "(ch 1, sc, ch1) 3 times" means that you will chain one, work one sc, and then chain again three times for a total of six chains and three scs.

Parentheses often set off or clarify a group of stitches to be worked into the same space of stitch. For instance, "(dc, ch2, dc) in corner sp".

[ ] Brackets and ( ) parentheses are also used to give you additional information.

Terms

Front Loop – This is the loop toward you at the top of the crochet stitch.

Back Loop – This is the loop away from you at the top of the crochet stitch.

Post – This is the vertical part of the crochet stitch

Join – This means to join with a sl st unless another stitch is specified.

Finish Off – This means to end your piece by pulling the cut yarn end through the last loop remaining on the hook. This will prevent the work from unraveling.

Continue in pattern as established – This means to follow the pattern stitch as it has been set up, working any increases or decreases in such a way that the pattern remains the same as it was established.

Work even – This means that the work is continued in the pattern as established without increasing or decreasing.

CROCHET TERMINOLOGY

The patterns in this book have been written using the crochet terminology that is used in the United States. Terms which may have different equivalents in other parts of the world are listed below.

United States	International
Double crochet (dc)	treble crochet (tr)
Gauge	tension
Half double crochet (hdc)	half treble crochet (htr)
Single crochet	double crochet
Skip	miss
Slip stitch	single crochet
Triple crochet (tr)	double treble crochet (dtr)
Yarn over (yo)	yarn forward (yfwd)
Yarn over (yo)	yarn around needle (yrn)

CROCHET HOOKS

Buying a crochet hook can be confusing because of the way crochet hooks are marked. Different manufacturers use different markings—some use a letter system, others use a numbering system. The most accurate way to choose a hook is to go by the millimeter (mm) sizing, which refers to the hook's diameter. Here is a guide from the Craft Yarn Council of America.

Mm Size	Letter Size	Number Size
2.25 mm	B	1
2.75 mm	C	2
3.25 mm	D	3
3.50 mm	E	4
3.75 mm	F	5
4.00 mm	G	6
4.50 mm	—	7
5.00 mm	H	8
5.50 mm	I	9
6.00 mm	J	10
6.50 mm	K	10½
8.00 mm	L	11
9.00 mm	M or N	13
10.00 mm	N	15
12.00 mm	O	—
15.00 mm	P	—
16.00 mm	Q	—
19.00 mm	S	—

GAUGE

This is probably the most important aspect of crocheting!

Gauge simply means the number of stitches per inch, and the number of rows per inch that result from a specified yarn worked with a hook in a specified size. But since everyone crochets differently—some loosely, some tightly, some in between—the measurements of individual work can vary greatly, even when the crocheters use the same pattern and the same size yarn and hook.

If you don't work to the gauge specified in the pattern, your afghan will never be the correct size, and you may not have enough yarn to finish your project. The hook size given in the instructions is merely a guide and should never be used without a gauge swatch.

To make a gauge swatch, crochet a piece that is about 4" square, using the suggested hook and the number of stitches given in the pattern. Measure your swatch. If the number of stitches is fewer than those listed in the pattern, try making another swatch with a smaller hook. If the number of stitches is more than is called for in the pattern, try making another swatch with a larger hook. It is your responsibility to make sure you achieve the gauge specified in the pattern.

MAKING FRINGE

Cut a piee of cardboard about 6" wide and half as long as specified in the instructions for strands, plus ½" for trimming allowance. Wind the yarn loosely and evenly lengthwise around cardboard. When the card is filled, cut the yarn across one end. Do this several times; then begin fringing. You can wind additional strands as you need them.

Single Knot Fringe

Hold the specified number of strands for one knot of fringe together, then fold in half.

Hold the project with the right side facing you. Using a crochet hook, draw the folded ends through the space or stitch from right to wrong side.

Pull the loose ends through the folded section.

Draw the knot up firmly.

Space the knots as indicated in the pattern instructions. Trim the ends of the fringe evenly.